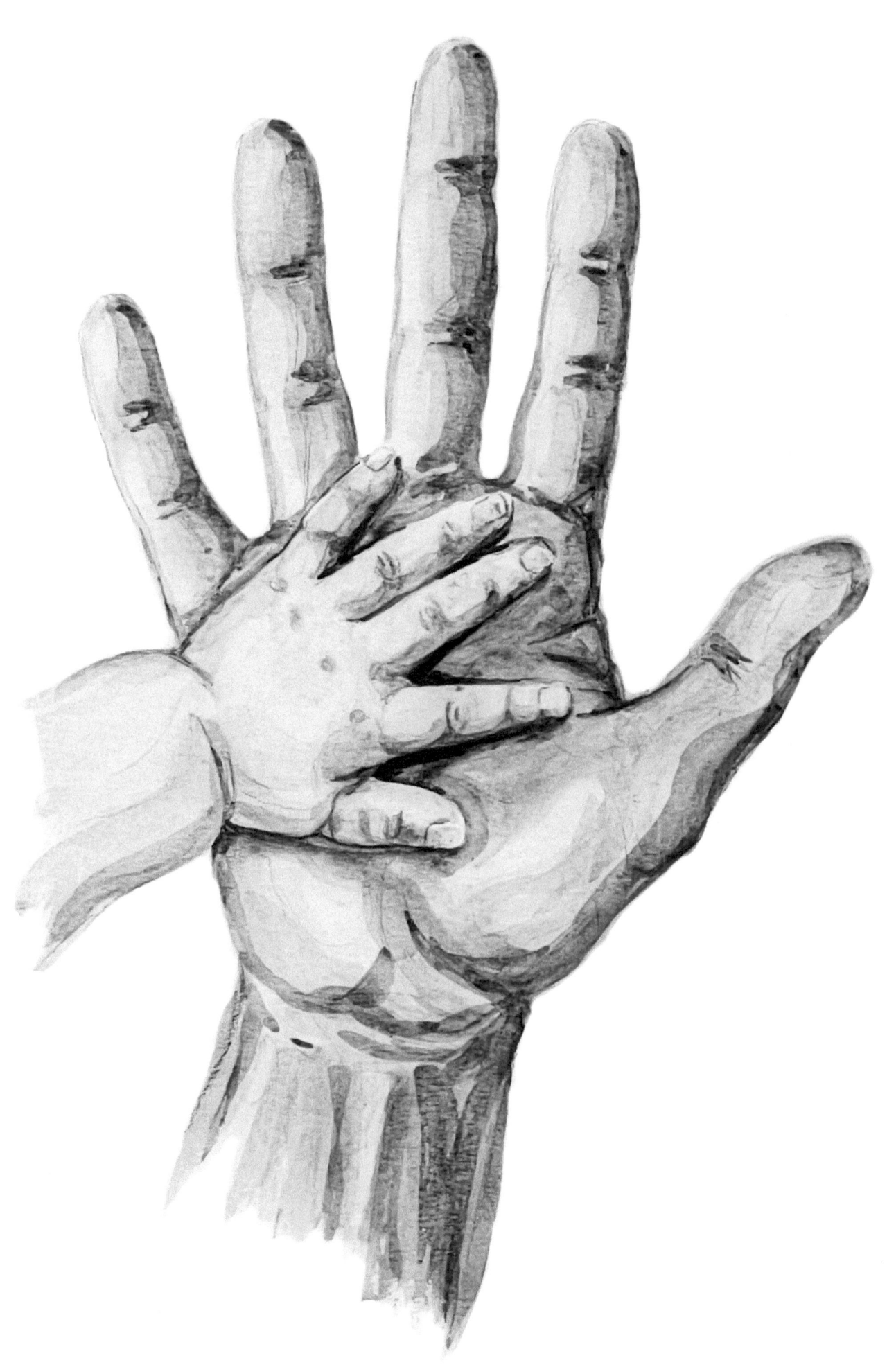

# Before You Were Here

For my daughters.
Dad loves y'all.
-Isaac


To the greatest gifts I've been given: my parents, children (Kyle, Audrey, John, Mark & Victoria), grandchildren, and my husband, Steven. With love and gratitude.
-Merrie

Before you were here,
next to me,


This is how you
came to be.

You came from love, from Daddy and Mommy;

Growing inside her beautiful tummy.

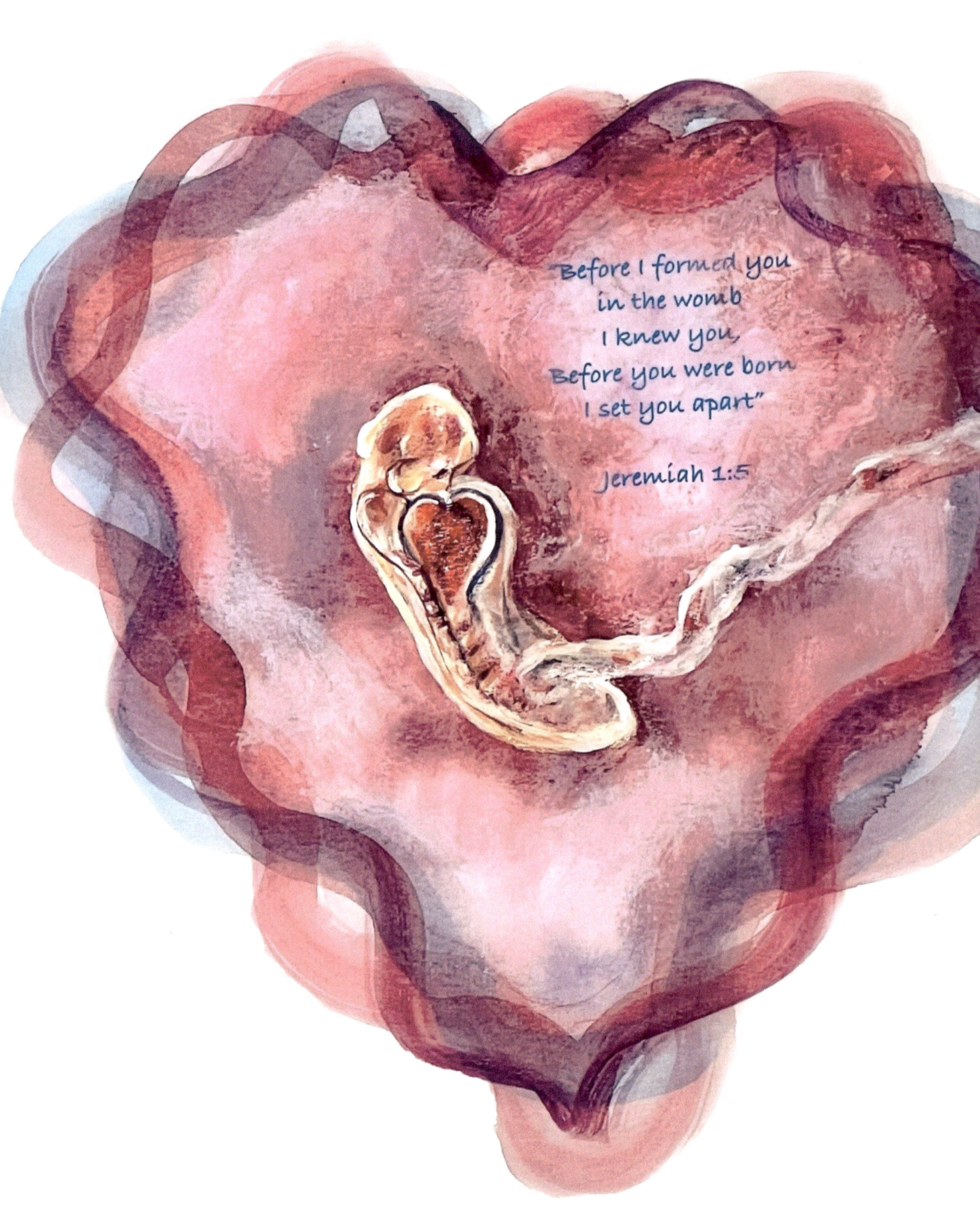

It didn't take long for your growth to start;

After only three weeks, you developed your heart.

When another week rolled around,

Your brain and spinal cord could be found.

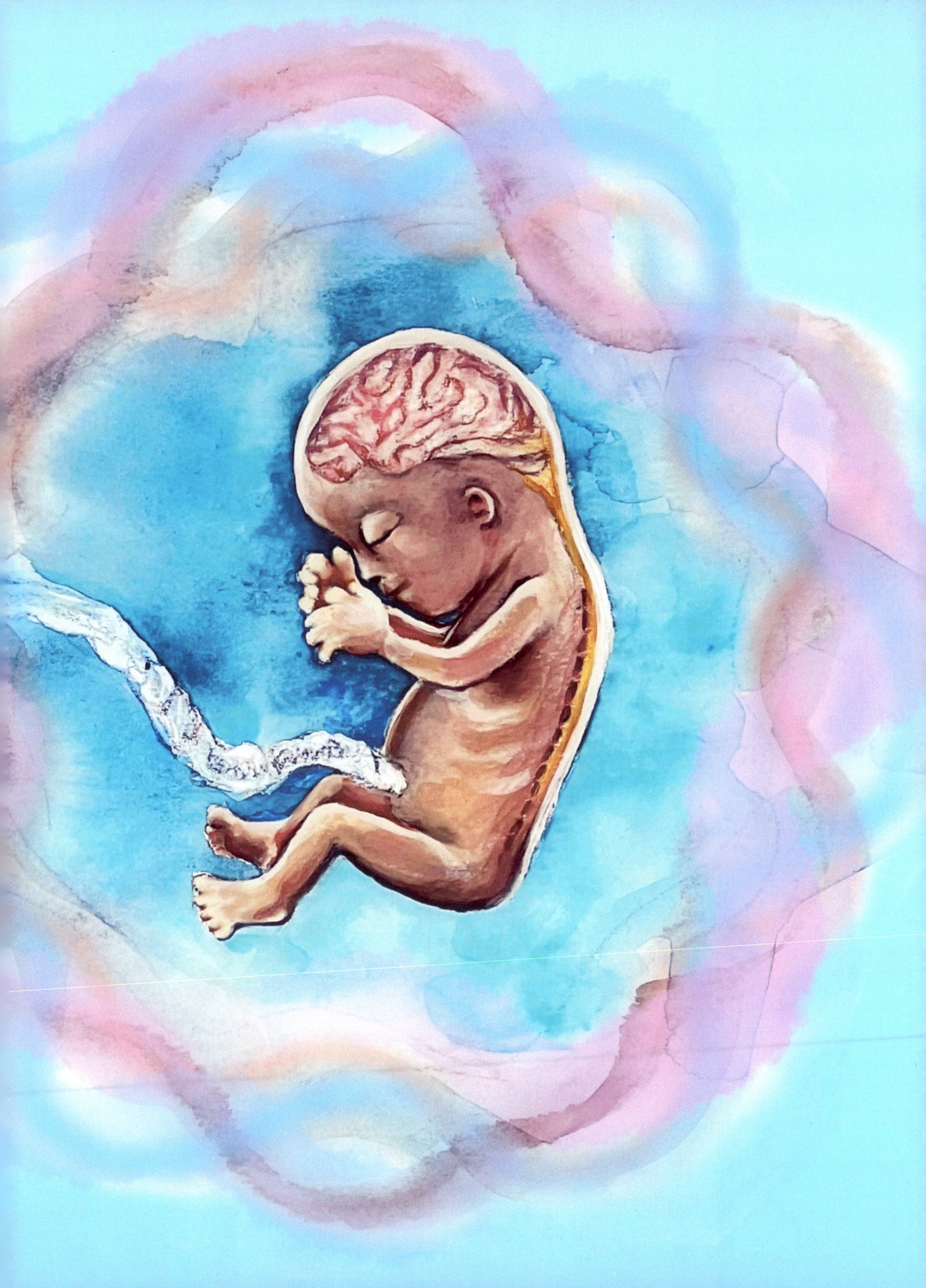

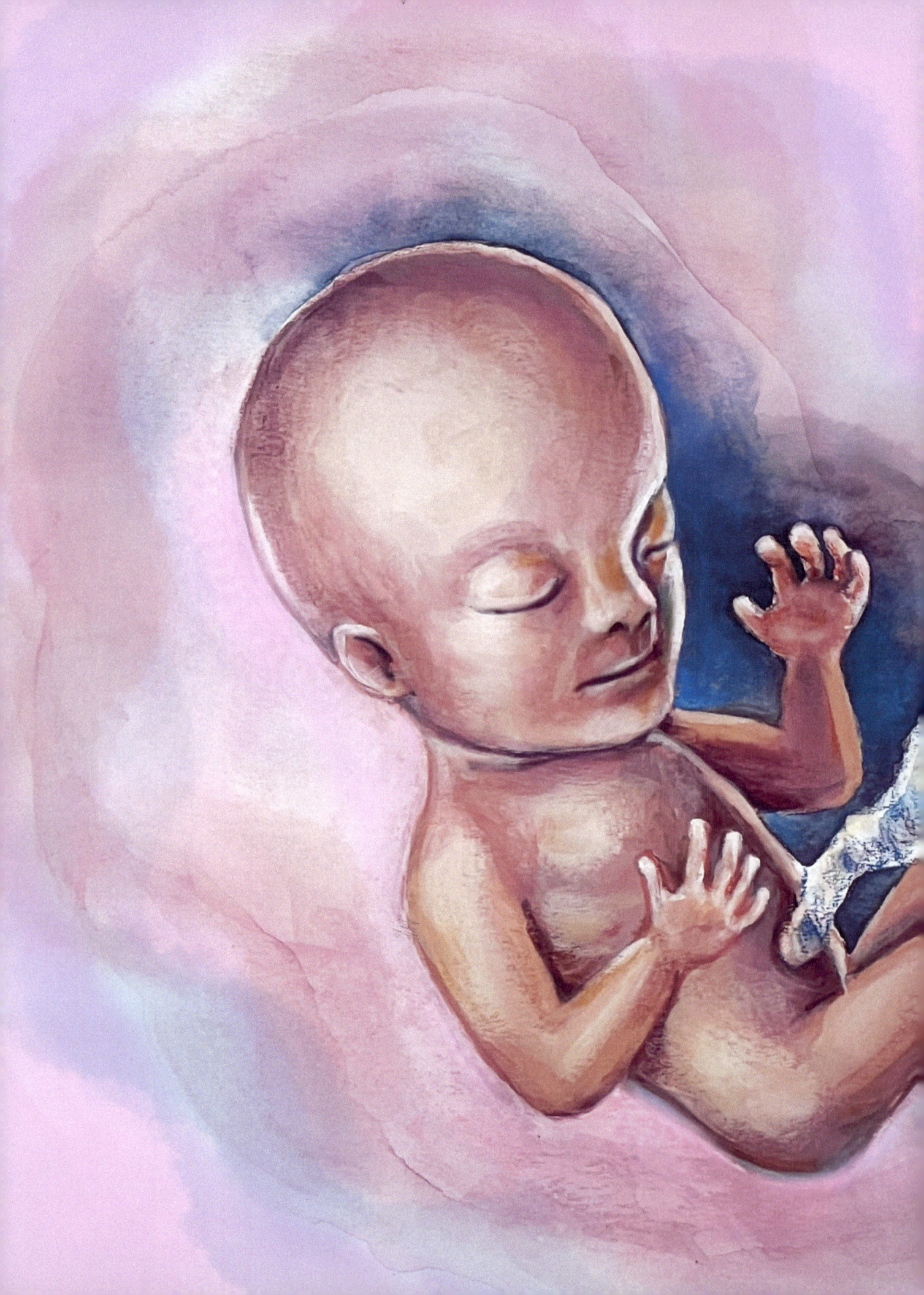

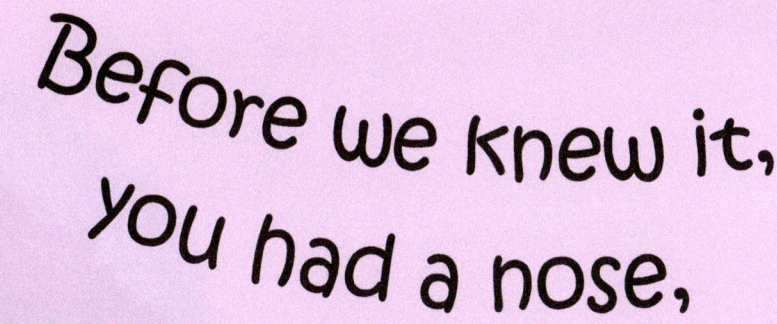

Before we knew it,
you had a nose,

Ten little fingers,
and
ten little toes.

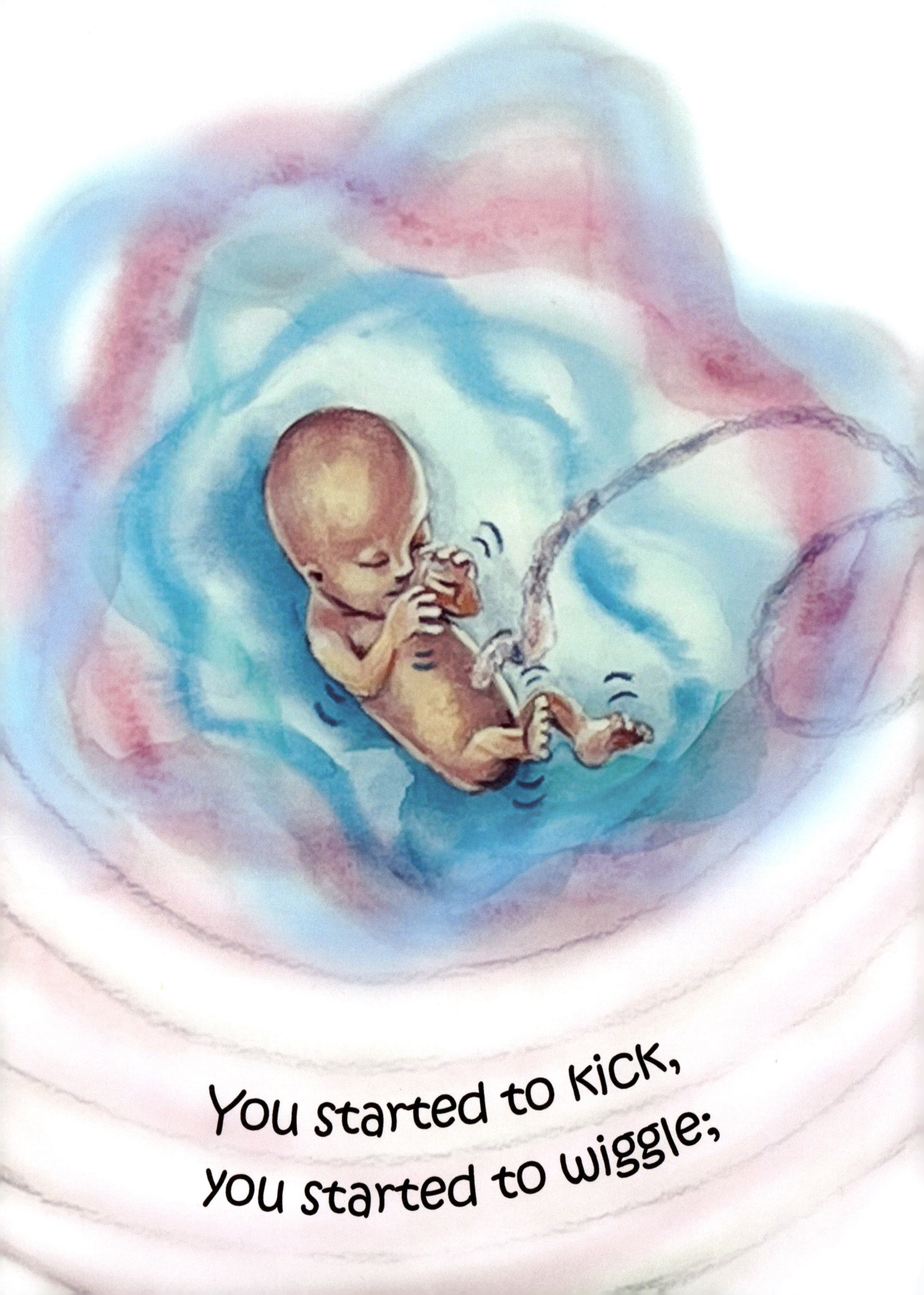

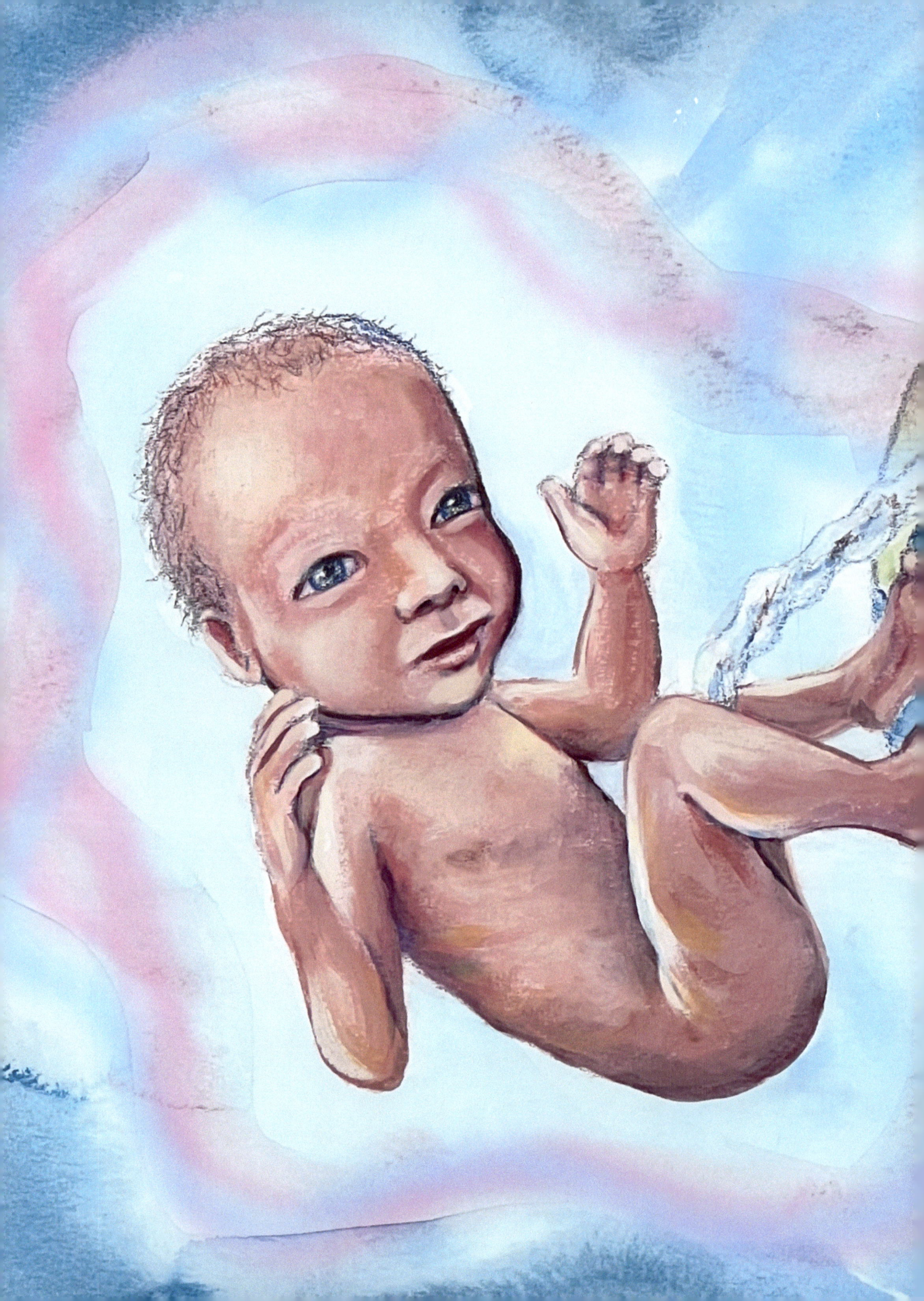

Last, you kept growing more and more,

Getting ready for a world to explore.

So before you were here, next to me,

You were fearfully and wonderfully made, you see.

Loved by God and loved by me,

You're exactly who you were meant to be.

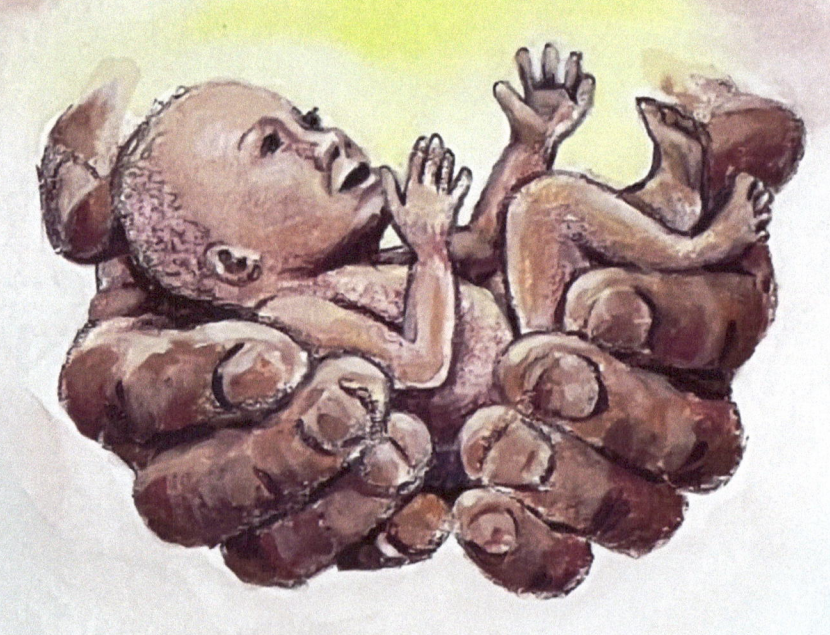

www.ingramcontent.com/pod-product-compliance
Lightning Source LLC
Chambersburg PA
CBHW040725060526
44119CB00083B/326